Pathways to Early Literacy Series:
Discoveries in Writing and Reading

What Changes In Writing Can I See?

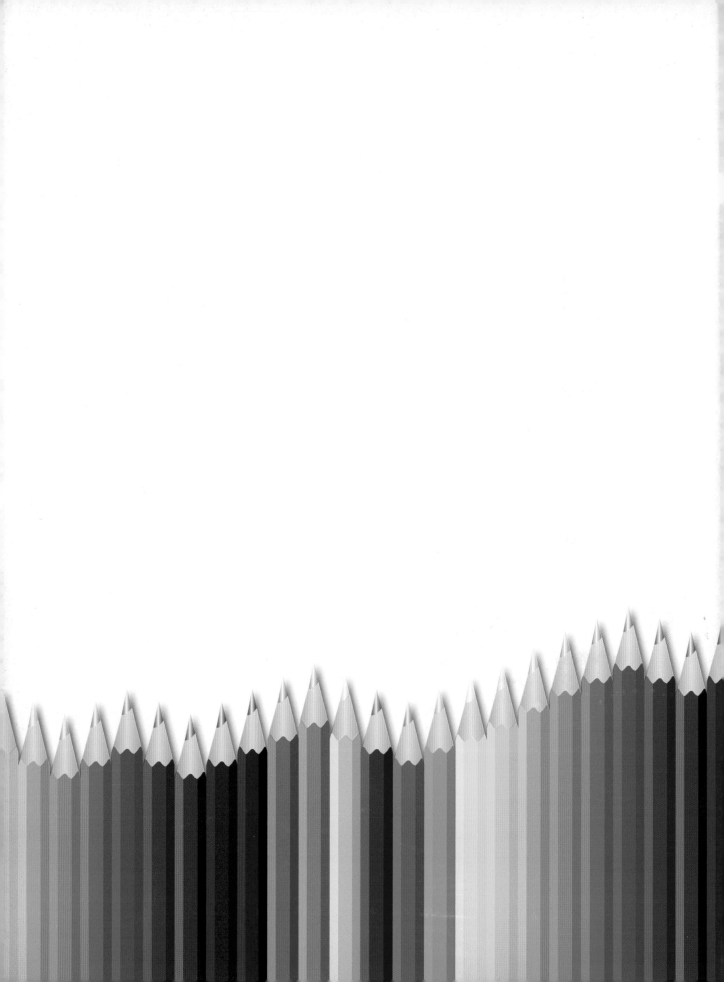

What Changes In Writing Can I See?

One in a series of books for parents, caregivers, and teachers of preschoolers and new entrants

Heinemann

Marie M. Clay

Cover photograph: Interact images (Shutterstock Images)

www.pearsoned.co.nz

Your comments on this title are welcome at
feedback@pearsoned.co.nz

Pearson
a division of Pearson New Zealand Ltd
67 Apollo Drive, Rosedale, Auckland 0632, New Zealand

Associated companies throughout the world

© The Marie Clay Literacy Trust 2010
First published by Pearson 2010
Reprinted 2012 (x2)

ISBN: 978-1-4425-3947-1

Printed in Malaysia via Pearson Malaysia (CTP-VVP)

Editor: Mary Anne Doyle, Ph.D., Professor, University of Connecticut and Consulting Editor, The Marie Clay Literacy Trust
Text and cover design: Cheryl Rowe, Macarn Design

                Library of Congress Cataloging-in-Publication Data
Clay, Marie M.
  What changes in writing can I see? / Marie Clay.
      p. cm. — (Pathways to early literacy series)
  Includes bibliographical references.
  ISBN-13: 978-0-325-03406-5 ((pbk.) : alk. paper)
  ISBN-10: 0-325-03406-0 ((pbk.) : alk. paper)
  1. English language—Composition and exercises—Study and teaching (Early childhood). 2. Language arts (Early childhood). 3. Language acquisition. I. Title.
  LB1139.5.L35.C548 2010
  372.62'3—dc22
                                2010017452

United States: Heinemann, 361 Hanover Street, Portsmouth, NH 03801-3912.

The editors and publishers thank the following individuals for their assistance with this book: Billie Askew, Christine Boocock, Dorothy Churchwood, Jann Farmer-Hailey, Patricia Kelly, Rosalie Lockwood, Carol Lyons.

The pronouns 'she' and 'he' have often been used in this text to refer to the teacher and child respectively. Despite a possible charge of sexist bias it makes for clearer, easier reading if such references are consistent.

Contents

Series overview

This book is one in a series of three written for parents, caregivers, early childhood teachers, and teachers of children in their first year at school. No set order is intended. Each book offers unique discussions and suggestions, and each can be read independently; it is complete in itself.

What Changes in Writing Can I See? introduces ways of keeping records of early writing. It describes how easy it is for parents and teachers to assess the changes taking place in children's writing by using everyday observations and by making more formal assessments.

How Very Young Children Explore Writing introduces the reader to the fascinating writing attempts of preschool children.

The Puzzling Code discusses how puzzling the written code is for young learners beginning formal reading instruction and offers instructional recommendations for supporting the child's complex learning.

A preschool teacher comments on a young child's writing:

> *I thought it was just scribble. But it isn't — if you*
> *understand what it is you are looking at!*

This teacher is correct. If you understand a little about what the child is trying to do when he writes, you can celebrate with him and tempt him to explore a little more about writing. Why is this helpful? Any of a preschool child's early attempts to write, however slight or fragmentary they may seem, are very beneficial for his ongoing literacy development. The child who experiments with writing before he goes to school has the opportunity to discover new concepts and ways to express ideas in print. Praise from an observant adult encourages him to keep extending his new-found ability. This freedom to make trials and errors with adult approval is the best preparation I know of for learning to read and write proficiently in school.

An introduction to the series: My perspective on relevant issues

Early writing experiences

My perspective is that children's early writing experiences provide them with powerful learning opportunities that support the reading and writing instruction they will encounter once they enter school. As they write their earliest messages, children gradually begin to make links between speaking, reading and writing. They may discover that:

What I say, I can write. And, what I write, I can read.

In the process of writing, they also learn many concepts about written language. For instance, they form understandings about letters and words, make connections between sounds and letters, and learn how to move left to right across the page. These discoveries are more beneficial to literacy learning than singing the alphabet or parroting rhymes about letter sounds. This raises the question of what is the place of phonics in reading instruction for our youngest learners.

When children begin to write little messages, lists, and other snippets of writing, parents often wonder whether they should teach phonics, or letter sounds, at home. I ask parents to just not buy into that idea. Think about it. In the phrase 'the phonics fad' what sounds do the letters 't', or 'h,' or 'p' have? What sounds would be the correct responses for each of the letters 'a, e, i, and o' in that phrase? Most English letters are used for more than one sound, so my questions are very confounding. When something happens often in a language, we think of it as a rule; however, many letter-sound correspondences in English break the rules, and that is very confusing for young children.

I agree that a reader has to learn to relate the sounds he speaks to the visual symbols of the writing system, but I assert that for the preschool child there is no better place to start than by helping him to write his personal messages. What I explain in this series of books is that instead of trying to teach children rules about our language (rules which are right only part of the time), we encourage them to speak their messages aloud (making the sounds), and we help them to write these messages.

Whenever I see or hear the advice 'you must teach your child phonics to prepare him to be a reader', I am reminded that this call has returned to education five times in my long life — twice during my school years and in three movements since then! Each time, phonics has been rejected as the royal road to reading because it doesn't take care of half of what the young child needs to know. Links between letters and sounds are very important, but a good literacy programme teaches much more. *Attending to the sounds made by letters in a word is a valuable but small part of what a reader has to know.*

At school, children begin the long task of linking sounds (what they say) with symbols (letters). Very quickly, they get the idea that there are regularities in letter-sound correspondences and the order of letters in words they read and write. But they also meet many irregularities when the 'rule' does not work.

One particular task that children do have to learn is how to listen to single sounds in the flow of their speech. This is a difficult task as individual sounds within words are quite hard for a young child to hear. Psychologists and linguists call this learning 'phonemic awareness.' To locate a particular sound in your own speech means learning to 'hear' one small piece of a larger speech pattern. Only then can you link the sounds to squiggles in print, the letters. Children take a couple of years to learn to hear the distinct sounds in what they say. However, once this learning is accomplished, they can hear most sounds, even the hardest examples, and the teacher's continued attention to phonemic awareness is not needed.

I have recently read well-designed research studies of advanced three- and four-year-olds who have taught themselves to read. The researchers show that these children could not pass the phonics tests commonly used by many school systems, and they did not 'sound out words' when they read. They have taught themselves to read *without learning phonics*, and researchers are still trying to find out how they do this. On the other hand, I know of no published research which shows that when any group of preschoolers has been taught 'phonics', it is the sole reason why they read well when they go to school. That belief is unsupported by evidence.

When we follow a very young child who is exploring print and trying to find out 'what is possible', we discover that he is trying to do something very complex. He starts by giving initial attention to the bits that are easy for him. Complex things are learned slowly, and each child shifts gradually from doing very simple things to doing very complex things. In young children's writing, it is that slow kind of learning, shifting week by week, that I advise parents and teachers to watch for, encourage, and celebrate. It may not always seem easy to be the observer rather than the participant, but it is often in children's little, self-chosen, spontaneous writing efforts that you can catch them in the act of discovery. That is when they are most likely to turn to you to share the joy of their achievements. There is no finer reward.

Individual differences resulting from early experiences

I have an unusual view of new entrants to school. They remind me of butterflies. Just as a butterfly emerges from a chrysalis, the school entrant is emerging from years of earlier development. He has learned to talk, and he has also seen print in his home and community. What each child chooses to attend to is very individual. Each arrives at school with his own set of understandings — his 'known'. This means that each child tends to know different things than other children about how we can write down what we say. A teacher cannot assume that all her children have similar understandings or knowledge. Each child's preschool literacy experiences and opportunities are personal and uniquely his own.

I take the view that instead of trying to teach children to work on small pieces of language, like letters and sounds, and a few words or sentence patterns, a good starting point is the child's own speech, its sounds, words, and sentence structures. He brings this knowledge to school. The task is to show him more about how his speech can be written down in new reading and writing tasks and how to expand speaking, reading, and writing outwards from there.

It is impossible to explain to young, preschool children how what we say is written down. The instruction and any directions from adults are beyond their understanding. You should therefore avoid trying to talk about it. Instead, chat about the purpose of your writing (the shopping list, the deposit form completed at the bank, the birthday card for grandad) and draw attention to the print around you in the home or the local environment (like stop signs and cereal packages). When you are writing, you can encourage children to join in the activity, like both writing a letter to grandma. You can also help them notice when people write and why they write.

Preschoolers today are aware of computers in the home and have often had experience in using them if only to play a computer game. They also may have watched older members of the family compose text messages or send emails. But this cannot take the place of learning to write. The activity of handwriting presents the two-fold challenge of physically forming the written letters and words as well as composing the messages in the mind. So it is vital that children also see adults engaging in handwriting for a variety of purposes. Above all, give children opportunities to make their own explorations in writing. If you can put together little writing kits of recycled paper of different kinds along with enticing pencils and crayons, and perhaps make a special space where the child can write at any time he chooses, you will channel his urge to write and need not worry about scribbles on the wallpaper!

I encourage you to be sceptical, critical, and thoughtful about any 'regimes' for teaching writing before school and any edicts about avoiding writing with preschool children. Instead, allow yourself to become fascinated by the ways a child's writing and his attention to print change through the years, particularly from age three to six.

How can adults support young children's attempts to write? This series of books provides an introduction to this fascinating topic, explores a variety of different approaches children may have to writing, and offers a range of recommendations.

1 | Observing change

It is exciting to watch how young children change. We notice the new things they master and proudly report each new development or undertaking. We are pleased to see when a child gets it right, or does something new successfully.

To observe a change, you have to notice what has been happening before that change occurs. Let me explain. The most exciting views of change come because first, you noticed the unsuccessful effort, then you noticed the 'nearly got it' attempt, and finally you celebrate because the child can do it (whatever it is)! So I strongly recommend that you watch the child's attempts to write and note how the child's attempts change as he gradually works out how things are done. Children's writing efforts and products are fascinating and very individual. By collecting many samples of writing over time and by becoming a sensitive observer, you will be able to see what changes in writing occur.

Adults may think of many occasions they have watched children closely. Here are two examples. These observations do not relate to writing, but they show a parent noticing new milestones.

The first child is only 18 months old. She is outside near the barbecue, and the screen door to the house seems to be shut. She wants to go inside. Unobserved and unaided, she toddles over to the door, up the step, and reaches for the door handle. She changes hands trying to open it, rattles the door, twists the handle this way and that, and tries again. Then, because it was never properly shut, she manages to get the door open and goes in: a new accomplishment, solved without help!

The second child is aged about two years. He is walking with his mother through the bush approaching a hut with a couple of wooden steps up to the open door. The top step slopes outward, as they often do. He runs ahead of the family, takes in the first step, and then steps on to the top sloping step. He sways precariously, about to fall, thrown by the sloping surface. He regains his balance, and then he stands with two feet on the top step and sways back and forth two or three times deliberately, testing out 'how one balances oneself,' before he scampers inside.

These two events were fleeting moments of change observed by a parent. Such observations of change allow us to describe developments in many areas of emerging skills, including writing.

Parents often chat about their young children's current interests and many similar observations. Some parents want to help their children begin school with a flying start. They ask, 'How can we provide opportunities for learning to take place?'

Teachers in preschool centres are interested in knowing how children are responding to the activities they provide. Many preschool administrators ask, 'Are we providing good opportunities for early literacy?'

Parents and preschool teachers will find that careful observation of each individual is most helpful in addressing their concerns and in describing children's writing performance and development. This is because there is no fixed sequence of learning in early writing that all children will or must follow. Therefore, *for preschool children and new school entrants we get a better sense of progress by watching the individual child before, during, or after a change in his writing.* This is best accomplished by collecting many pieces of writing on an ongoing basis. This collection, when looked at closely, allows us to describe changes in the individual child, which is the most important information for supporting ongoing development in our preschool writers.

Once children have been at school for about a year, we can compare any child's progress with the average progress of other children of his age. We might do this in order to offer extra attention to those who are getting left behind, but that approach is *totally wrong for preschool children.*

Young preschool children learn about literacy in haphazard ways. They have odd and various encounters with print in their daily lives. Some take no notice of written language. Others take an interest for a while and then 'go off it' and ignore it. Some nudge their parents and siblings constantly and through their questions they learn a great deal. Are there any ways to look for progress in such very different children?

Yes, there are. It helps to look at a child's early learning in two ways, involving reading and writing. To provide examples, consider the responses to the following two questions regarding reading and writing.

How does this child look at books and respond to stories?

Children learn many concepts about print by being read to by adults or older siblings. They discover that pictures carry the story and that text is related to the picture. They may learn that the print carries the message. Over time, they may look at books respecting rules of our written language, including reading the left page before the right and moving left to right across lines of text. Note when your child makes these discoveries.

When does his scribble/drawing turn into trying to write?

Children's early attempts to write indicate that they are aware of using signs (the special code) to communicate messages. We may recognise some of the letters, and we may see some inventing as the child creates his unique way to accomplish the writing task. These early attempts to write suggest that the child appreciates how to represent language in written form. Below you see Nina's first attempt to write the alphabet. This is her invented code.

If we think about those two things, then watching for progress in early literacy learning is as easy as keeping height and weight graphs to monitor a child's physical growth.

This book describes ways to watch for the changes that occur in a child's pretend writing and awareness of print (observed in either their writing products or their 'reading' of books). Having observed the changes and made some record, the parent, or the teacher, can weigh up what new activities and opportunities may support the child's ongoing development.

There are many paths to early literacy

Compare the examples that follow and think about the differences among preschoolers on early literacy learning. There is no single measuring tape you can use. They do *not* all do the same things at about the same time.

Little children choose where to direct their attention. Quite naturally, they begin to make their first attempts to write because of what they notice in everyday life at home and when they go out into the community. Their family members and other people around them affect what they notice, as the following examples suggest.

In February a little girl was writing Christmas cards. Her mother suggested Easter cards. But no! She insisted they would be Christmas cards. (Let it go, Mum. It is a reason to write even though it is out of season.)

One boy, not interested in writing, saw his father copying something out of a book. After that, he was often seen pretending to copy out of books. Here is his illustrated version of Cinderella.

Nina made her shopping list. It has a purpose and different items must be written in different ways. At this time Nina almost always writes from right to left! The second word is 'chocolate because it is a big word,' she said. (Very observant. And she is only three and a half years old!)

By the time Nina gets to school she is trying to remember to write from left to right, and she writes an apology to her school teacher aunt for reversing the writing on her birthday card. She wrote 'Sorry Aunt Jo, I forgot to do it the school way.'

Children develop differently

Literacy development occurs as a result of opportunities available in the child's day-to-day activities, and these may be surprisingly different. Expect each child's development to be unique, a reflection of his experiences.

The same discoveries occur early for some and much later for others, as happens with teething, walking, and talking. We do not want to put young children into a training schedule for play which says you must learn this before that. This notion of a schedule for learning will become the common practice only when the child starts formal schooling.

If you provide an environment full of interesting possibilities for imaginative play, and then step back, letting children choose where to direct their attention, you can expect surprising new discoveries to be made. So follow the child's lead, support their efforts, and enhance their experiences. The outcome is new learning.

When the child shows you that he understands that print carries a message, he has reached a very important stage. Surprise! Before they get to school, most children are fantastically successful at catching on to this basic idea. Messages they have heard spoken can also be put down on paper. Of course, you may not be able to read your young writers' messages because they don't use the correct code signs. But they will read them for you.

Few children at the age of five will not have tried to work this out. There will always be the Mary or Johnny who steadfastly chooses to ignore those opportunities until it is time to start school. And that is OK. If we push too hard and children become concerned, that could create anxiety which does not help learning.

Briefly, let me share a few suggestions for parents that will encourage and support writing opportunities for their preschool children. (See *How Very Young Children Explore Writing*, another title in this series, for more suggestions.)

Put aside a special box for attractive scrap papers and provide the child with a writing tool 'on demand'. Encourage any interest. It will be momentary, lasting just a few seconds at first. Stay around and watch, and then put the materials away. The child's interest will gradually increase, and it will then deserve a little more of your attention. Before long you will be invited to share the writing or to provide examples to be copied. Nudge them into writing from time to time when they have a real purpose for it.

Be aware that a developing interest in print can show up in any one of many places.

This list provides a small range of possibilities. You and your child will find many more.

- The child may learn something from a favourite book.
- The 'M' for McDonald's hamburgers may catch Jena's eye.
- Jimmy may claim that a particular letter is 'his' letter because it is in his name.
- Tim might ask where to begin to write on a page.
- Sarah may want you to write something for her to copy.

She may ask you to let her scribble on your letter to her Grandma.

He may surprise you by noticing something unexpected, such as Dylan, who found familiar letters on his dad's computer keyboard.

Capture the changes that occur

Once the child has become interested in writing, parents can begin to capture samples that over time show change and progress. However, a quick glance at the child's writing will not provide you with food for thought to describe change clearly. You need to take a very close look.

'Observing closely' means paying careful attention to everything that is happening. An important first step is the collection of information about the child's writing experiences and attempts. Following are a range of ways to begin to collect and organise a chronology of a child's early writing.

1 Collect and save drawings and bits of writing

To help you gather many samples of writing, have a box, or special bag, in a handy place and drop in scraps of writing left lying around. Make time to record the date. Congratulations, you are now capturing progress!

2 A little notebook

Keep a notebook and pencil within easy reach. What have you noticed? Make a quick note of what you see, because it is so easy to forget. Also, because the interest may turn up only now and then, capture it immediately. Add to your notes when you notice another attempt. Put in the date, as in the samples from several parents that follow.

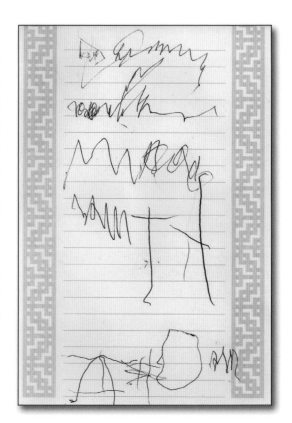

Thomas wrote his first note! He wrote to Uncle Rich explaining 'I came to see the garden and I wish you were home.' (Written August 17).

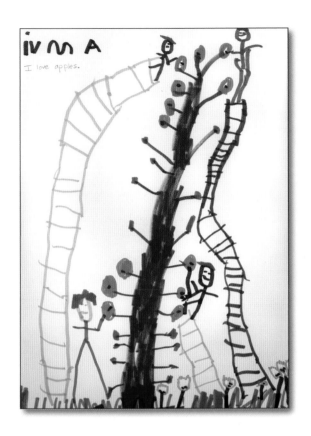

I love apples.

Jonathan enjoys drawing and talking about our family. Finishing his drawing of family members picking apples, he spontaneously wrote and said: 'I love apples!' (Written October 10.)

My family is special to me.

Colleen's mother kept a number of samples over several months. Note the changes in Colleen's writing.

Colleen drew her family and read her message: 'My family is special to me.' (Written July 16.)

Colleen's messages are beginning to show her awareness of the initial sounds in words. This is a change from her presentation of strings of letters. (Written October 20.)

Colleen's stories reveal more awareness of letter sounds and the appropriate use of upper and lower case letters. (Written November 22.)

3 The blank jigsaw

An alternative way to record observations is to fill in a special form created for parents by a group of researchers (Weinberger, Hannon, & Nutbrown, 1990). Working with parents of preschool children, they asked them to make an entry on a blank jigsaw puzzle every time they saw their preschool child attempt something different with marks and signs, or written language. It is quite surprising how quickly the spaces on the jigsaw will get filled up with notes of things your child has done or commented on.

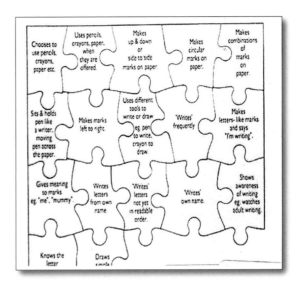

4 Read diaries that mothers have kept

I have found that we can learn by reading parents' published diaries of preschool children's literacy activities. Two indepth diary records kept by mothers for research projects describe early writing and reading that they observed in their young, American children. Both books are readable, and the samples of work are of particular interest.

- Marcia Baghban made a case study of a child from birth to age three entitled *Our Daughter Learns to Read and Write,* published by the International Reading Association in 1984. It is mainly about scribbling, but it shows how scribble changes over time.

- Glenda Bissex called her book *Gnys at Wrk: A Child Learns to Write and Read.* The title includes a message written by her five-year-old son and pinned to his bedroom door. She studied his writing development from preschool through the early school years. It was published by the Harvard University Press in 1980.

These diaries suggest to me that I should be cautious about any conclusions I draw from my own observations, because learning about writing is a very complex task. I know this. Yet I do encourage parents to collect interesting samples of their children's attempts to make sense of the signs of written language.

5 Read widely

Recommend any articles about early writing that you find to your friends. Such sharing of information among parents is a beneficial way to expand everyone's understandings, discover new ways to engage children in writing and support their opportunities to learn.

Preschool writing and learning

Once a child has begun to explore writing, there are many new features that might emerge, even if the writing is a long way from 'real' writing. 'Pretend writing' is very necessary learning. Through this phase a child sorts out what you can and can't do when you put messages into print (using a code to write speech down). Codes have many hidden rules.

- Messages are conveyed in print (in code).
- Messages may take several lines of print.
- Messages are composed of words.
- Words are collections of letters.
- Words and letters are used repeatedly.
- The placement of the letters and words is important (the space between words).
- All printing must go left to right.
- The starting point and movement on the page are critical (from top to bottom).

New understandings can lead to further discoveries within days, and this may be followed by a period when nothing new appears. And actually, it takes quite a long time before correct spellings and letter formations appear.

I won't talk about the different types of changes that you might see, just because the changes are made at different times by different children and appear to be unrelated to age. Some children start early and make a lot of progress before they go to school. Others start to notice writing only when they enter school.

How much children know at school entry about learning to write will depend very much on how much interest, or lack of interest, they had in writing before entering school. While interest seems to be a critical factor, talent and ability do not. The children who notice writing only when they enter school engage in a catch-up exercise to get to 'real writing.' Within the context of classroom instruction, learning and change do come very quickly.

First year teachers who have learned to be sensitive observers of children's writing are well-prepared for respecting individual differences in the first months of school. They understand that instruction leads development, and they work with individual children in ways that do not demand too much or too little from them. They also provide the support and models young writers need to be successful in their many attempts.

Knowing the influence that a child's interest in learning about writing has on what they know at school entry, I encourage parents and preschool teachers to take special interest in early writing. At home and in preschool settings, adults can plan opportunities for young children to explore print and writing in their play.

Exploring leads to copying and more

From scribble to circles and crosses to that first, clearly distinguishable letter, children's attempts to write get bolder. For a long time, the young child's ability to copy will only change slowly. Adults expect to make a letter and have a little child copy it correctly almost immediately, but it is not as simple as that. If there is a sequence of changes, they run something like this. The child will:

- Scribble above, below, around, or on your model.
- Make invented forms scattered on the page.
- Trace over what you wrote.
- Copy a letter or two above or under yours.
- Copy your model, a complete word or sentence.

Some shapes (letters) are easier to make, while others have angles and are so difficult that the child will not try them for a long time. (The diamond shape is notoriously hard until after six years.) The angles on the letter 'k' are troublesome to some. Does the child have an easy name to write or a hard one?

Look at the samples below from two children who have just begun school. Both drew a picture and told a story about it. Yet, we can see a very important difference. The teacher wrote down the dictated story, showing how a writer writes.

The sample on this page shows a young writer who has copied the teacher's model, not perfectly, but good-for-age. On page 26, we have a sample of a child who is at an earlier stage. He makes no attempt to copy. Any attempt he subsequently makes will mark a change in his writing behaviour.

Young writers often find copying tasks fatiguing and hard to sustain. Consequently, they switch to inventing, generating the letters, words, and messages of their written language. This is not a backward step: inventing is another way children can discover concepts about writing.

My study of early writing suggests that the first things children learn are gross approximations which become refined over time. Their primitive letter forms, invented words, and pretend messages evolve into appropriate forms and clear, readable messages.

7 Putting aside the search for correctness

Adults must put aside a search for correctness. We will miss some important changes if we start by looking only for correct learning or performance. It is quite common for teachers, parents, and evaluators to attend only to what is correct about what a child does. That is unhelpful, and I will try to explain why.

Think about watching for the first steps a child takes. Those first steps come after the baby pulls himself up, stands, falls, and tries again and again, *before* he steps out alone. We readily understand all that as progress towards walking. The same thing happens with learning to talk. We cannot predict exactly how and when walking or talking will emerge. Both improve gradually and at different ages, and that is what we have learned to expect.

We help babies through crawling and standing, cooing and babbling, and we demonstrate walking and talking all the time. Of course we do! I recently held two babies who were about three months old. One replied to my talking with talking noises, the other just listened. These children were very different in their responses to my language. We expect such differences, and we know that it does not mean that one will necessarily begin to talk intelligibly before the other.

While providing opportunities for babies getting ready to walk and talk, we anticipate imperfections, stumbles, or 'errors'. We do not expect the child to make discoveries without errors, and we often interpret and celebrate their errors as evidence of significant learning.

The study of oral language provides many examples. Young children's comments, like 'I see two cats and two mices,' or 'I goed to Grandma's house yesterday,' indicate that the speaker has discovered rules for making nouns plural (cats, mices) and for expressing past tense (goed). Even though his utterances aren't perfect, his 'errors' reveal that he has acquired important understandings. Correctness will come with time and experience, and more opportunities to engage in conversations with others.

Learning about written language proceeds just like that. A little child begins to take an interest in what parents or siblings or other writers do when they write or read. Writing is easier than reading for the child to observe and imitate. It is not nearly so obvious what a person is doing when he or she is reading, whether aloud or silently. Watch the beginnings of children's writing before they take their first 'real' steps. As sensitive observers, you will see the child's progress and strengths while looking beyond any errors.

Can I make an analysis of preschool writing?

I have encouraged collecting many samples of children's writing over time, from the first scribbles to their attempts to record or generate letters, words, and messages. We can look closely at their samples, including pages of 'pretend writing', to assess their development and describe their current understandings and known bits of information such as their personal set of familiar letters.

To help focus your evaluation and develop a more thoughtful analysis, you may use the following questions. Practice by referring to Jenny's sample of 'pretend writing' below, or take any recent piece of writing from a young child you know. You will notice it helps to observe the child during his writing so that you also have a record of his comments and questions.

Questions to guide the analysis of early writing samples

- List the real letters the child knows or forms correctly. Count them.
- Did he say anything about the letters, such as 'That's for ball', or 'That's in my name'?
- Sum up. Does the child know very few, about half, or most of the letters of the alphabet?
- How does the child work on the page (left to right, right to left)?
- Record any comments the child makes. Often he will tell you about a problem he had and how he solved it.
- Make a note about unusual things — layout on the page, or speed of working.
- Do you have unanswered questions? Share them with someone.

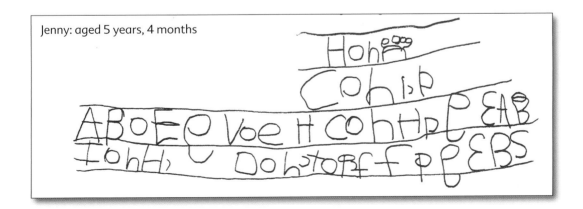

Jenny: aged 5 years, 4 months

What you have discovered is quite hard to sum up! Perhaps these additional questions about Jenny's writing may help:

1) Was she copying?
   No.
2) Was she using letters she knew to make new letters?
   Very possibly.
3) Was she listening?
   Cannot tell. It does not appear that she was.
4) Was she looking for shapes?
   Possibly.
5) Was she trying to control her writing hand?
   Yes.
6) Was she inventing something new?
   Yes.

Here is a summary of Jenny's writing:

Jenny appears to have control over some of the rules of written English. She is aware of using letters repeatedly to construct many words, and her words appear to form a message (or pretend message). Her message may contain one or more sentences. She forms 16 letters correctly (H, h, O, o, A, B, C, E, e, c, f, I, t, S, V, p) and writes with a mix of upper and lower case letters. She demonstrates awareness of the directional patterns applied to printed language, including writing from left to right across a line, with a return down to the left. It is not clear that she understands that spaces are used to separate words. She does not appear to have any known words that she can write, nor does she appear aware of letter-sound correspondences.

The analysis of Jenny's writing suggests she is very focused on letter formation and production, and that she has many strengths. She has discovered and is using important concepts about writing messages. As Jenny continues to 'write messages', she may soon demonstrate new awareness. This is an exciting time to watch for her next discoveries, remembering these will come on her time schedule, not your own!

Completing the analysis and summary, you will have a report of the known sets of letters, words, and concepts (for example, moving left to right across the page) that the child displays. These are his or her strengths in writing. This is useful information for parents to share with new teachers, or for teachers to share with one another.

Observing and noting such strengths means that you will be spotting the young shoots from which more skill will grow. A child's code-learning will expand out of his or her current strengths.

Your questions will be different if the child you are observing is attending to words and messages. We need another set of questions to search out how the child is thinking.

Questions to guide the analysis of early written messages

- Is the message a complete sentence? Or several sentences?
- Does the child write words in the message from left to right?
- List the words written correctly. Count them.
- Does the child copy or request words?
- Do any invented words reveal attempts to represent sounds heard in words correctly (for example, writing 'ane' for any)?
- Are any sounds in words represented correctly with consistency (for example, the first sound in words, or the last sounds in words)?
- Does the child make some well-formed letters?

The questions to guide the analysis of a written message focus on the *message*, *words*, *sounds*, and *letters*. These are four aspects of written language that the writer/reader handles at the same time as he works on texts. Our youngest writers will attend to one and neglect the others. It takes a long time for them to be able to attend to all at the same time.

In the next example a four-year-old ignores the printed code on the page she is writing on. She focuses on creating a message from a copy provided by her older brother.

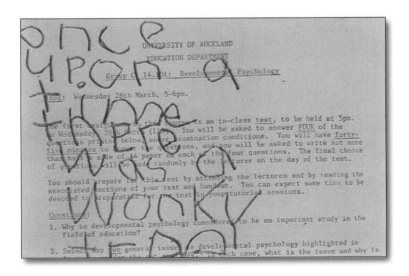

And in contrast the next example is from a child who finds she can hear the first letter of every word.

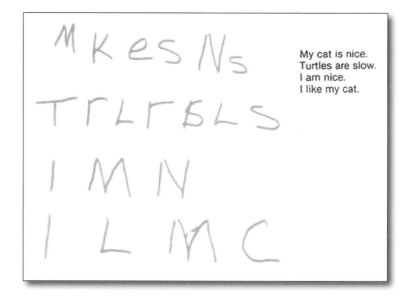

My cat is nice.
Turtles are slow.
I am nice.
I like my cat.

Here is a clear message written by a young child who was critically evaluating my 'Concepts About Print Test'. I had deliberately created some printing errors, and she was able to detect them. Achia dictated the letter to her teacher and signed it. This young child has learned enough to make a critical appraisal of a non-conforming text!

Dear Marie Clay,

You messed up the pictures in your book called Stones One was upside down. You also put the words upside down and mixed up the words.

I think you should fix the book. I like the book that way after it's fixed up.

Thank you,

Achia Fisher

Achia Fisher

The child begins to use a language code as a baby, babbling and trying out his first words. It takes about five years before he faces the noises and sounds of oral language in written form. The human brain is apparently specially designed to do the first set of learning but is not particularly well-tuned to work with written codes.

Each child has to programme his own brain to match speech to squiggles on a page of print. In school he learns to work at high speeds, putting symbols on paper that others can read with their eyes. Achia has made that complicated shift.

A group activity for teachers in training

Gather some examples from your preschool writers (or use the examples below). Discuss with your group what you notice about each child's writing. Fine tune your personal observations by listening to what other group members notice. You will discover how much you can learn from children's early attempts to write.

A group of teachers could discuss questions like those listed in the previous chapter or more general ones like 'How do you know when a child is on the brink of a new writing discovery?' Build up a list of things about print which are rules (or conventions) that must not be broken if we are to make sense of a language code.

- Make a start by telling each other what you think each writer in the examples knows about the code. Put what you observe into words.
- Discuss one thing about the written language the child is aware of. Would you do anything about that? Why, or why not?
- Discuss one thing about written language the child is not aware of. Would you do anything about that? Why? Why not?

The children's stories are:

My mom (mum) is shopping.

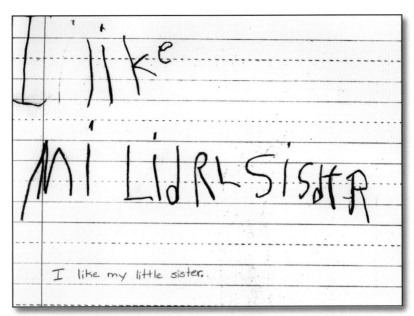

I like my little sister.

I love ice cream.

An invented story.

I am going to decorate my tree.

The rain ruins my day but I still like it.

The transfer from early childhood settings to school

Many authors have written about the need for early childhood educators to pass on to the school the developmental information they have about children making the transition to primary education. Professor Stuart McNaughton has emphasised this in his studies of children from other cultures entering a school where only one language is used in teaching (see McNaughton, 1995 or 1999).

What does it mean when someone recommends that the early childhood teacher should pass a portfolio of children's writing to the new entrant's teacher? It means that both educators must be aware of and understand the development of early writing prowess before and after entry to school, at whatever age that is.

So, what is 'a portfolio' and how would that help? In *Effective Literacy Practice Years 1 to 4*, a text for teachers of the first four years of school, a portfolio is described as a 'cumulative file of work, especially writing' (Learning Media, 2003, p. 65). Dated examples of a child's work are collected to demonstrate what the child is aware of, how he is thinking, and particularly, starting points for further learning. Also documented are any existing confusions — a path along which the child has recently travelled, and in what way he is prepared for taking new paths ahead. The sampling procedures described in this text fit this need and purpose.

Very importantly, the former teacher gives the present teacher the benefit of her interpretations of the child's work. So the early childhood educator has to know the child well and comment in some detail on what she believes she has observed. A summary statement like, 'He can write his name and a few other things', is not enough!

This is where discussions between teachers — within preschools and schools and across both — would be helpful. The school teacher has to understand what the preschool teacher has been observing. For the young child this is a time of change, spurts in progress — and also, at times, confusions, setbacks, and misunderstandings. Transitions like this are most important times in a child's development. Teachers who are sensitive observers will be able to support the young learner as he adapts to new ways of literacy learning.

More formal assessments of writing performance

Once children have entered school and are developing as readers and writers, there are a number of procedures that are helpful to guide the teacher's assessments of their performance and progress. I will describe several that I have found useful for assessing children's writing samples and early reading concepts.

Writing Samples: Rating written expression

To estimate the level of a young child's written expression in the first six months of instruction, take three samples of his written work on consecutive days, or over a period of two weeks. Apply the scale below to rate the three aspects of the writing task representing areas that must develop as the child's written expression evolves: Language Level, Message Quality, and Directional Principles. This is an arbitrary scale and should be taken only as a rough guide to a child's instructional needs (also detailed in Clay, 2002, pp. 99-100).

If you are tempted to use only one or two samples you must be aware that your one sample may not have captured the child working at peak level. It might even have been a really bad day, or he might have been trying to do something very new and not succeeding. Taking three samples will give you a better estimate of where his competencies lie.

Rating the young child's written expression

A LANGUAGE LEVEL: Record the number of the highest level of linguistic organisation used by the child in his three records.

1 Alphabetic letters only.

2 Word or words (any recognisable word).

3 Word group (any phrase of two words or more).

4 Sentence (any simple sentence).

5 Punctuated story (of two or more sentences).

6 Paragraph story (at least two themes).

B MESSAGE QUALITY: Record the number below for the best description of the child's sample.

1   He has a concept of signs. (Uses letters, invents letters, uses punctuation.)

2   He has a concept that a message is conveyed. (He tells you a message but what he has written is not that message.)

3   A message is copied, and he knows more or less what that message says.

4   Repetitive, independent use of sentence patterns like 'Here is a . . .'

5   Attempts to record his own ideas, mostly independently.

6   He produces a successful composition.

C DIRECTIONAL MOVEMENT: Record the number of the highest rating for which there is no error in the sample of the child's writing.

1   No evidence of directional knowledge.

2   Part of the directional pattern needed is known:
   • Start top left.
   • Move left to right.
   • Return down left.

3   Reversal of the directional pattern (right to left and/or return down right and move to the left.) A sample with one lapse should be rated at this level.

4   Correct directional pattern.

5   Correct directional pattern and spaces between words.

6   Extensive text without any difficulties of arrangement and with reasonable spacing of words in text.

Recording

You can record your ratings on a simple table like this one. Children with similar profiles could be worked with in a group.

	A Language Level	B Message Quality	C Directional Movement
Not yet satisfactory	1-4	1-4	1-4
Probably satisfactory	5-6	5-6	5-6

Here is an example of the use of the rating scale on Miranda's written expression. Three samples, the rating, and a summary statement are provided. Her written stories say:

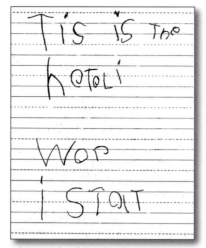

This is the hotel where I stayed.

I like flowers. They are so beautiful.

I am a ballerina. I am the best ballerina ever.

The rating of Miranda's writing

Language Level	4
Message Quality	5
Directional Movement	5

Summary

Miranda's writing samples were collected over eight days. She is currently writing complete sentences and using interesting language. She has begun to write two-sentence stories; however, she does not seem to be aware of punctuation. She writes independently using a sound analysis to record unfamiliar words (for example, Fawrs for flowers; Budfl for beautiful; Balowena for ballerina; sTaT for stayed). She knows a few basic words in detail (for example, I, a, is, the, like, so). She understands directionality and uses appropriate spacing. She writes using a combination of upper and lower case letters; she forms some letters well.

Miranda displays strengths on all three dimensions: Language Level, Message Quality, and Directional Movement. Her writing of longer messages of two sentences is a new development. She will benefit in demonstrations of how to punctuate her sentences. Ongoing instructional support of hearing sounds in words, forming all letters correctly, and continuing to build the core of words she writes without a copy will also benefit her.

Writing Vocabulary Task: The words he can write

The Writing Vocabulary Task offers an inventory of all the words a child can write. This task is particularly suitable for the school age learner, and even those children who read or write very little are able to respond to the task. (This task has also been developed for Clay's (2002) *Observation Survey of Early Literacy Achievement*.) Directions for administering, scoring, and interpreting the task are as follows.

Administration

Directions for administering the task involve the following statements and questions for the child. This is a 10 minute task. First, give the child a blank sheet of unlined paper and a pencil and say:

> *I want to see how many words you can write.*
> *Can you write your name?* (Pause and repeat if needed.)
> *Can you write your name?*

Start timing the child at this point.

- If the child says 'No', ask him to write some letters, and then say:

> *Do you know how to write is, to, I, or am?*

Usually, if a child does not try to write his name, he will not know many other words.

- If the child says 'Yes', to your question about writing his name, say:

    Write your name for me.

- When the child has finished his attempt (good or not), say

    Good. Now think of all the words you know how to write and put them down on this paper for me.

Prompt the child to keep trying. He will slowly think up other words to write. The words he gets wrong give you valuable information about how he is thinking.

When the child stops writing or needs prompting, suggest words that you think he might know how to write. Work through a list of words such as *the, in, at, am, on, up, and, go, look, come, here, this, me, he, mother* or *mum, dad, car, . . .*

Continue until you feel sure the child's writing vocabulary is exhausted, or stop after 10 minutes.

Very able children need little prompting. Keep the hesitant ones trying for as long as interest holds, and then end the task.

Scoring

Each word completed accurately can be marked as correct and receive a score of 1, without penalty for poor letter formation. If a child accidentally wrote a word that was correct but read it as another word, or did not know what it was, it is scored as an error. Words written in mirror image are scored as correct only if the child actually wrote the letters in the correct sequence. Progressions such as look, looks, looked, looking, or cat, sat, fat, mat, hat are allowed as separate words.

Interpretation

Some children cannot produce a single word. By five and a half years, many children can write five to seven words, and by six years of age most children can write many words. But how many depends on cultural things like opportunities, interest, early childhood education programmes, and the child's curiosity about the written code.

A record of the development of one child's writing vocabulary can be taken at intervals in the first two years of school, and the progress can be very interesting. Children can be grouped for instruction according to the level of their competence in early writing and in other kinds of competencies described earlier which affect both reading and writing.

8 August   (5)

mark

To I am a

---

4 December   (33)

mark   go   look

going   The   is
I   am   a   me

He   we   uq

                    come
to   here   in
Zoo   my

it   beg This   looks

for   ho   looking
book   be   books
took   like   hook   Said
            bike   mike

The sample above demonstrates Mark's growth in writing vocabulary knowledge from August to December of his first year of school.

12

Particular observations you might like to make

An additional set of informal techniques that allow teachers to observe the child's writing attempts and his attention to print include the following writing and reading tasks.

- Put a cross on the right hand side of the page and ask the child to write some words for you (his name and a few known words). Then put the cross on the left hand side and repeat the directions. Compare the results. This set of directions sometimes produces mirror writing.

- Present the child's name in a three-piece puzzle cut so that the pieces fit together in any order (Clay, 1991). Jumble the pieces and ask the child to make his name. You will be able to see what the child is noticing about his name and what things he is not yet noticing. Consider the beginning, the end, and the middle of the word or name.

    /Na/ /th/ /an/   /Sa/ /mu/ /el/   /Sh / /ar/ /on/

- Present a test of arranging print on a page. Give the child a small piece of paper and say: *Write me a long story on this page.* Notice what rules for writing messages he is paying attention to (for example, starting point, directional movement, return sweep to the left, and so on).

- Ask a child to point to the words of a simple, clearly written book as you read it to him.

- Ask questions about direction in either reading or writing: Where to start, where to go next, and where after that?

- Ask the child to read a very easy book of about eight pages or share a short story book with the child, once or twice. Then ask him to read it to you. Record what you notice in his reading behaviour.

The Concepts About Print Task

The Concepts About Print Task (Clay, 2000 and Clay, 2002) is not one I can present here, but it is an assessment that teachers of five- and six-year-old children find so helpful that I wish to make you aware of it and reinforce its usefulness.

The purpose of this assessment is to assess a child's understanding of basic concepts about our printed language. It reveals what the child has noticed from his experiences with print (including both the personal writing and book experiences he has had) and what he has ignored, or just not noticed. More specifically, it addresses what children are attending to, including where one starts to attend to the print in text, what direction one moves, and how one moves through a word. Teachers use the results of the task to identify the child's current understandings, the concepts to be taught, and any confusion to be untangled.

This task has travelled well across languages. One research study of English-speaking children showed it was a sturdy measurement instrument throughout the first year of school. It seems to work for any alphabetic language and is available in English, French, Spanish, Maori, Danish, Irish Gaelic, and Greek (languages written left to right) and in Hebrew and Arabic (languages written right to left).

You will need a short training course to use this assessment effectively. Ask someone who is trained to demonstrate it to you. Choose someone who understands 'good testing practice' to teach you to use this assessment. They would need to check on two things: how you work with children, and how you score and interpret what the child does.

After some practice you will be able to read the 'test story' to a child, asking him questions as you turn each page. If your training has been good, you will be able to rely on your results. You will see clearly which of the concepts about print the child already accepts and works with, and which ones have yet to be learned.

14 Summary

From my observations of many young writers, I conclude that there is no one sequence of development: Each child's path of discovery is unique. My research suggests that the types of shifts we might observe in early writing include the following:

- What is a sign? The child discovers the use of signs and uses many made-up symbols. His 'writing' may be lines and circles and crosses, with few recognisable letters.
- He learns and uses a few conventional signs (letters) and invents others. You can decide which are the letters and which are the inventions.
- He specialises in alphabetic letters and writes word-like strings of letters.
- He discovers that letters and words are repeated in messages.
- He is clear about the order of words in a message.
- He is clear about the left-to-right order of letters in words.
- He continues to make up (generate) personal signs, words, and messages.
- He writes multiple lines of text showing ability to use space appropriately (top to bottom; left to right, space between words).
- He engages in his own form of segmenting sounds in words by saying them slowly and recording what he hears.
- His letter formations become more conventional.
- He catches his errors of direction and word arrangement, and comments or corrects.

When we observe the changes that occur in early writing over a period of time, we find a chronology of development. From their opportunities to explore and follow their interests, children make great leaps forward in understanding concepts of our written language code. And when the child realises that messages we speak can be written down, he has gained the main concept for *reading and writing progress.* Parents and early childhood teachers make important contributions to the growth and eventual school success of preschool children by providing many opportunities to draw and write, by following each individual child's lead, by offering support and models, and by celebrating all of their attempts.

References

Baghban, M (1984). *Our daughter learns to read and write.* Newark, DE: International Reading Association.

Bissex, G (1980). *GYNS AT WRK: A child learns to write and read.* Boston, MA: Harvard University Press.

Clay, MM (1991). *Becoming literate: The construction of inner control.* Auckland: Heinemann.

Clay, MM (2000). *Concepts about print for teachers of young children.* Auckland: Heinemann.

Clay, MM (2002). *An observation survey of early literacy achievement.* Auckland: Heinemann.

Learning Media (2003). *Reading in the junior classes.* Wellington: Ministry of Education.

McNaughton, S (1995). *Patterns of emergent literacy: Processes of development and transition.* Auckland: Oxford University Press.

McNaughton, S (1999). 'Developmental diversity and literacy instruction over the transition to school' in JS Gaffney & BJ Askew (Eds.), *Stirring the waters: A tribute to Marie Clay* (pp. 3-16). Portsmouth, NH: Heinemann.

Weinberger, J, Hannon P, & Nutbrown, C (1990). *Ways of working with parents to promote early literacy development.* Sheffield: University of Sheffield Educational Research Centre.